CW00823350

Persian Sofreh
Heavenly Food Made Easy

£1.50

Persian Sofreh

Heavenly Food Made Easy

Fary S. Tehrani

The Book Guild Ltd
Sussex, England

First published in Great Britain in 2005 by
The Book Guild Ltd
25 High Street
Lewes, East Sussex
BN7 2LU

Design by Reza Sadr
Photography by Andrew Carruth
Portrait by Pedram Rasti

Printed and bound in Singapore under the supervision of
MRM Graphics Ltd, Winslow, Bucks.

A catalogue record for this book is available from The British Library

ISBN 1 85776 916 3

Dear friends

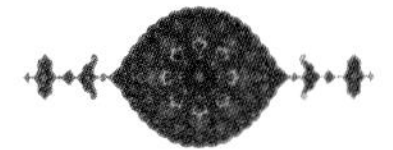

For years every time I had a dinner party or invited you over to a meal you have been so kind and complimentary and have asked for the recipe of the food that I had prepared for you, so I have been encouraged to make my recipes available for your use. I am very grateful for your encouragement and pleased that at last I am able to offer you what I promised. I know most of you are familiar with Persian food but I have tried to explain every recipe as if it is your first experience. I have named all the different dishes in Farsi and there are some ingredients that are named in Farsi, to make this book as original as possible. However, after each menu I have explained what the ingredients are and where to find them. A lot of our food is quite heavy and because of that it should be served with care so that the whole meal is not too heavy. Also certain foods are not really compatible with others. So, I have put together eighteen menus for a dinner for four to six people and five party menus and three for bigger parties. Obviously if you want you can mix and match to your own taste but be careful.

I would like to dedicate this book to the first admirers of my cooking, my two sons Nader and Pedram who have always been my inspiration and my incentive in life and for whom I have put so much love into my cooking and tried to perfect it. I hope you will have many happy parties and meals and this book will help you achieve them.

Happy cooking

Contents

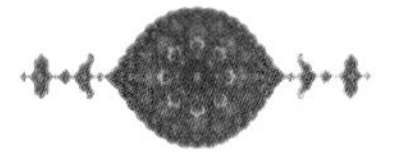

The guest is the beloved of God 4

Menus 7

Party Menus 45

Starters 57

Main courses 83

Desserts 121

Index 138

The guest is the beloved of God

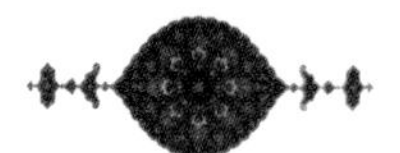

This is a famous phrase that is framed and displayed on the wall in almost all Persian houses. Persian hospitality is second to none in the world. Parents bring up their children to respect and honour older people and any guest that ever arrives in the house. It is the duty of the lady of the house to welcome the guests in and make sure that they are well looked after and made to feel at home; the first thing to do is to offer refreshment and food. Mothers teach their daughters to be always ready to welcome any invited or uninvited guest at any time, to not only share the food but also put the guest before themselves and serve them first. In most households there is usually more than enough to go round, but even the poorest family is very proud to offer whatever food or refreshment they have on their plate to God's beloved and make them their own beloved.

As a nation we are very proud of this heritage of love, hospitality, generosity and family values. In the old days before tables and chairs people used to have very large cushions that they put all around the room and for each cushion there was also one against the wall for the guest's back. These cushions varied according to the wealth of the owner from normal cloth to pure silk Persian carpets sewn on the front of the cushion. At mealtimes a large cloth called a sofreh would be spread in the middle of the room in front of the cushions and the food would be served on it. Even now the tablecloth is called sofreh. All the family sat round the sofreh three times a day and had a family meal; they would delay the meal and wait for every last member of the family to arrive to eat together. Mother would serve everyone and they would all wait until everybody was served before starting to eat.

On a Persian sofreh there is always a basket of fresh herbs, which consists of five to six different herbs with feta cheese, and flat bread is a must. Bread is baked in special clay ovens that are heated by burning wood and when the oven is hot enough they stick the dough that has been rolled and flattened on the wall of the oven. When it is ready, this most delicious bread is taken out with a long fork. Bread is served with every meal. Different pickles and jams, yoghurt, and salad are always present on a sofreh.

All the food is brought to the sofreh together and obviously the guest is served first and from the best part of the food, and asked repeatedly to have more; it is a great honour and considered a compliment if the guest has a second or third helping. After the meal is over, traditionally we have a basket of fruit, which varies by the season, and then Persian tea, which is tea leaves brewed in a teapot and served in small glasses that show the colour of the tea. Sometimes we add cardamom, saffron, fresh mint, or any other herb that is fancied to this tea. After a good Persian meal the most enormous appetites are normally satisfied, but if not there are always Persian sweets to offer God's beloved.

Menus

These menus were created to help plan a complete meal. Each recipe is designed to serve four to six people. For more guests you should double, treble or increase the quantity of the ingredients as you require. These menus have been selected carefully to make sure that the starter, main course and dessert are compatible and complement each other. Some of the starters can be served as hors d'oeuvres with the drinks before dinner, along with some herbs and olives.

All the ingredients that are used in Persian cooking can be found in any shops that sell Indian, Persian Middle Eastern and Arabic foods. The internet is also a good source for buying special ingredients.
In all the recipes using saffron, this needs to be soaked in about 2 tablespoons of hot water before use.

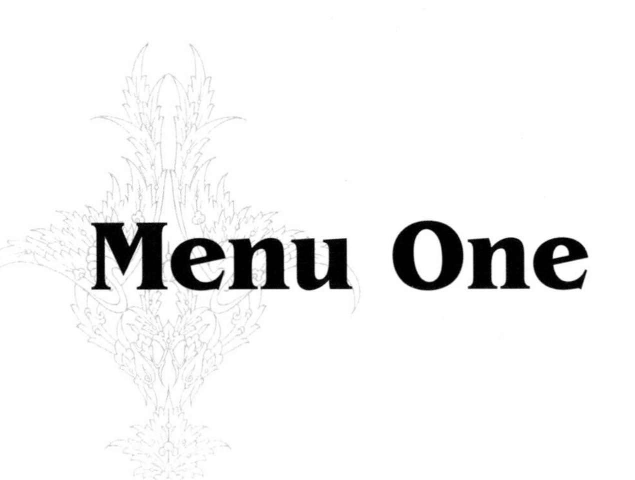

Menu One

Starter

Coocoo sabzi ⓥ (Page 68)
Mast-o-khiar ⓥ (Page 73)

Main course

Shevid bagali polo ⓥ (Page 94)
with lamb

Dessert

Fresh watermelon
Melon
Mango

Freshly brewed tea with mint

The herbs used in the starter in this menu are fresh parsley, coriander, dill weed and spring onions. In the main course rice is cooked with dill weed and broad beans.
A tray of fresh fruit is very refreshing after the meal.

Coocoo sabzi

Shevid bagali polo

Menu Two

Starter

Coocoo bademjan ⓥ (Page 65)

Mast-o-moosir Available ready made to buy

Main course

Geymeh bademjan (Page 105)

with polo (Page 84)

Dessert

Shirberenj (Page 127)

Freshly brewed tea with mint

This menu features aubergine, which is a delicious vegetable; mast-o-moosir is yoghurt with moosir, which is a cross between garlic and onion. Khoresh-e-geymeh is aubergine and lamb. Shirberenj can be served with honey, jam or just icing sugar.

Coocoo bademjan

Menu Three

Starter

Onion soup Ⓥ (Page 69)

Main course

Zereshk polo Ⓥ (Page 88)

Saffron chicken (Page 102)

Dessert

Fresh mango

Ice cream

Zoolbia (Page 122)

Freshly brewed Darjeeling tea

Zereshk is a very small red berry that is sour and has a very nice flavour; this dish is sweet and sour mixed rice, served with saffron chicken. For the dessert zoolbia is a very crunchy sweet that can be served with tea.

Zereshk polo

Menu Four

Starter

Borani-e-bademjan ⓥ (Page 62)

Panir-o-sabzi (goats cheese & herbs)

Main course

Loobia polo (Page 98)

Tandoori chicken (Page 118)

Dessert

Nan-e-khamehi (Page 132)

Fresh fruit

Freshly brewed leaf tea with mint

The starter in this menu is made with aubergine and yoghurt; loobia polo is rice with string or French beans and lamb or beef. Dessert is éclairs with fresh cream or crème anglais.

Tandoori chicken

Menu Five

Starter
Ash-e-mast (Page 58)

Main course
Sabzi polo Ⓥ (Page 86)
Mahi (Page 87)

Dessert
Cream roulette (Page 134)

Fresh coffee with cream

Ash is a traditional Persian soup, and here we serve it with yoghurt. Sabzi polo is rice with fresh herbs, which are coriander, parsley, spring onion and dill. This is served with fried fish with saffron. Sabzi polo mahi is the traditional menu for the Iranian new year's day.

Cream roulette

Menu Six

Starter

Halim bademjan (Page 76)

Main course

Eslamboli polo Ⓥ (Page 100)

Chicken in tomato sauce (Page 103)

Dessert

Spicy apple dessert Ⓥ (Page 126)

Chinese tea

Halim bademjan is a favourite starter, and it contains kashk, which is concentrated yoghurt that is dried, but can be bought in a jar like creamy yoghurt. Eslamboli polo is rice with cubes of meat and aubergine. Spicy apple is a very light sweet that can be served with cream.

Halim bademjan

Menu Seven

Starter

Ash-e-jo (Page 59)

Main course

Tahchin-e-bademjan (Page 91)
with chicken

Dessert

Sholezard Ⓥ (Page 128)
Ice cream

Freshly brewed Mint tea

Ash-e-jo is Iranian soup made with barley instead of rice, and it can be served with yoghurt or fresh lemon juice. Tahchin is a delicious and decorative food and can be made with chicken or lamb. The dessert is a very special dish that is served at special celebrations and we use a lot of saffron in it. Can be served hot or cold.

Tahchin-e-bademjan

Menu Eight

Starter

Coocoo sabzi ⓥ (Page 68)

Main course

Sabzi polo ⓥ (Page 86)
Mahi (Page 87)

Dessert

Shirberenj (Page 127)

Fresh fruit
Tea or coffee

This is the traditional new year's day menu for the Iranian new year on the 21st of March. The starter uses fresh herbs and for the main course the fish is served with fresh lime. Dessert can be served with fresh strawberries or jam.

Coocoo sabzi

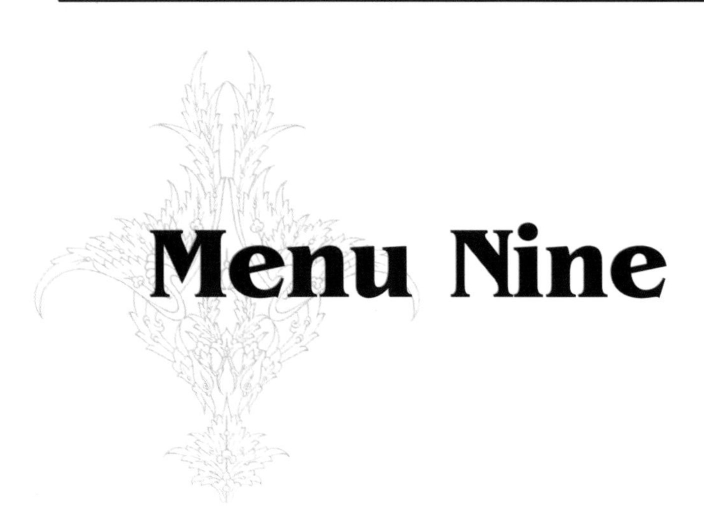

Menu Nine

Starter

Koofteh-e-shevid bagali (Page 70)

Main course

Khoresh-e-gormeh sabzi (Page 113)
with polo (Page 84)

Dessert

Tarhalva ⓥ (Page 136)

Saffron tea, freshly brewed

Some people serve Koofteh as a main course, but here we have Koofteh shevid bagali as a starter made with broad beans and dill. Khoresh-e-gormeh sabzi is made with parsley, coriander, spring onion and dill. Tarhalva or Halva is another traditional dish and is very popular.

Khoresh-e-gormeh sabzi

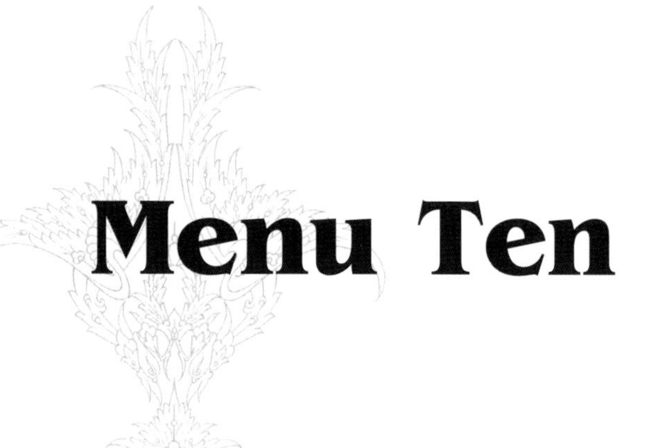

Menu Ten

Starter

Borani-e-esfenag Ⓥ (Page 63)

Main course

Koresh-e-bademjan (Page 107)
with polo (Page 84)

Dessert

Spicy apple dessert Ⓥ (Page 126)
with ice cream

Freshly brewed hazelnut coffee

This menu starts with yoghurt with spinach and for the main course we have aubergine with lamb; to make it tasty we can add sour grapes to the khoresh just before serving. Spicy apple dessert is very refreshing with ice cream.

Koresh-e-bademjan

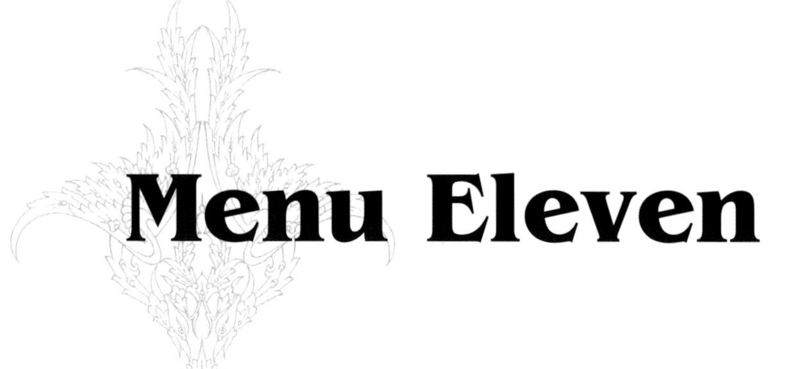

Menu Eleven

Starter

Chicken wings (Page 64)

Main course

Khoresh-e-loobiasabz (Page 106)
with polo (Page 84)

Dessert

Fereni Ⓥ (Page 131)

Tea or coffee

This menu starts with deep fried chicken wings, served with chopped chillies. Khoresh-e-loobia-sabz is made with French beans and lamb in a tomato sauce. Fereni is a light dessert that is made with milk and rice powder and can be served with fresh fruit or conserve.

Polo

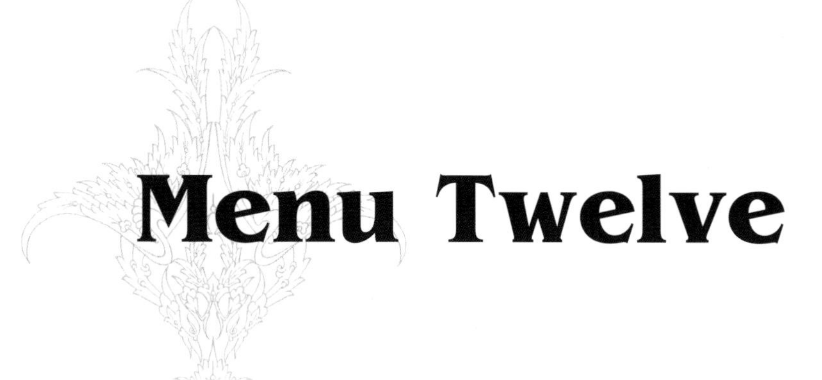

Menu Twelve

Starter

Borani-e-bademjan ⓥ (Page 62)

Main course

Khoresh-e-fesenjan (Page 110)
with polo (Page 84)

Dessert

Masgati ⓥ (Page 130)
Seasonal fruit

Coffee

Borani-e-bademjan is aubergine and yoghurt; if you like, it can be made very hot by adding chilli powder. Khoresh-e-fesenjan is chicken in a sweet and sour sauce that is made with walnuts and concentrated pomegranate juice and is served with plain rice. Masgati is a light sweet that can be served with tea or coffee.

Khoresh-e-fesenjan

Menu Thirteen

Starter

Shami (Page 77)

Main course

Khoresh-e-alooesfenag (Page 112)
with polo (Page 84)

Dessert

Tarhalva ⓥ (Page 136)

Herbal tea or coffee

Shami is a kind of cutlet, which is made with nokhochi powder (chick pea powder), and is a very delicious starter. Alooesfenag is made with spinach, lamb and prunes and served with plain rice. For dessert we have Tarhalva, which is made with flour, saffron and sugar.

Tarhalva

Menu Fourteen

Starter

Nargesi ⓥ (Page 74)

Main course

Koreshe-e-karafs (Page 108)
with polo (Page 84)

Dessert

Masgati ⓥ (Page 130)

Tea or coffee

Nargesi is an easy starter that is made with spinach and egg. Khoresh-e-karafs is celery in a parsley and mint sauce, served with plain rice. Masgati is a sweet that is made with arrowroot.

Koresh-e-karafs

Menu Fifteen

Starter

Halim bademjan (Page 76)

Main course

Shevid bagali polo Ⓥ (Page 94)
with lamb or chicken

Dessert

Yakh dar behesht Ⓥ (Page 137)

Lychees with ice cream

Halim bademjan is a delicious starter that some people serve as a main course since it is quite substantial. Shevid bagali polo is light and fresh; rice cooked with broad beans and dill weed and served with lamb or chicken that is cooked with butter and saffron. Yakh dar behesht means ice in heaven, and it is a light dessert that can be served with crushed pistachio nuts.

Shevid bagali polo

Menu Sixteen

Starter

Mast-o-khiar (Page 73)

Panir-o-sabzi (Cheese and herbs)

Main course

Chelo kebab

Barg and coobideh (Pages 114, 115)

Dessert

Zoolbia and bamieh Ⓥ (Pages 122, 123)

Sholezard Ⓥ (Page 128)

Mint tea

Chelo Kebab is everyone's favourite: it is plain rice and different kebabs, such as barg, which is made with lamb fillet, or coobideh, which is mince kebab or chicken kebab. For starters we usually have very light dishes and mast-o-khiar is yoghurt and cucumber with fresh mint, also a basket of fresh herbs (mint, basil, spring onion, radishes, or any other favourite fresh herbs) with feta cheese and served with flat Persian bread. For dessert in this menu we have zoolbia and bamieh which are both very sweet, and sholezard, which is made with rice and saffron.

Sholezard

Menu Seventeen

Starter

Cutlet (Page 78)

Panir-o-sabzi (cheese and herbs)

Main course

Adas polo Ⓥ (Page 96)

Saffron chicken (Page 102)

Dessert

Cream roulette (Page 134)

Cardamom tea

Cutlet is another starter that can be served as a main dish; it is made with mince and potatoes. The main course is rice with lentils and is served with fried dates and sultanas, complete with saffron chicken. Cream roulette is made with fresh cream and is very tasty. We always serve tea or coffee with the dessert.

Adas polo

Menu Eighteen

Starter

Kashk-e-bademjan Ⓥ (Page 66)

Mast-o-khiar Ⓥ (Page 73)

Main course

Kalam polo (Page 104)

Dessert

Sholezard Ⓥ (Page 128)

Mint tea

We start this menu with Kashk-e-bademjan, which is aubergines in a sauce of kashk (kashk is concentrated and dried yoghurt) and mast-o-khiar is yoghurt with cucumber and mint. Kalam polo is rice with chopped cabbage and mince with spices. Sholezard is rice cooked with saffron and almonds.

Kashk-e-bademjan

Party Menus

When organising a party the most important thing is the food, and deciding and arranging the menu can take a lot of time and effort. To simplify this I have prepared party menus and, for much bigger parties, feast menus to help you. We usually serve fresh salad, herbs with feta cheese, bread, butter, pickles, plain yoghurt, and cheese. These are almost always present on a Persian sofreh. A big party can be organised as a buffet and guests can help themselves to various dishes. In fact Persian food is very suitable for big parties, as it is so easy to increase quantities.

Party Menu One

Starter

Coocoo sabzi Ⓥ (Page 68)

Salad olivier (Page 60)

Mast-o-khiar Ⓥ (Page 73)

Main course

Khoresh-e-gormeh sabzi with polo (Page 113)

Shevid bagali polo with chicken Ⓥ (Page 94)

Dessert

Sholezard Ⓥ (Page 128)

Zoolbia and bamieh (Pages 122, 123)

Mint tea

Party Menu Two

Starter

Coocoo bademjan ⓥ (Page 65)

Shami (Page 77)

Green salad

Main course

Morasaa polo with chicken (Page 92)

Geymeh bademjan with polo (Page 105)

Dessert

Shirberenj (Page 127)

Spicy apple dessert (Page 126)

Tea or coffee

Party Menu Three

Starter

Halim bademjan (Page 76)

Cutlet (Page 78)

Mast-o-khiar ⓥ (Page 73)

Main course

Khoresh-e-fesenjan with polo (Page 110)

Khoresh-e-karafs with polo (Page 108)

Dessert

Nan-e-khamehi (Page 132)

Cream roulette (Page 134)

Tea or coffee

Party Menu Four

Starter

Coocoo shevid bagali (Page 81)
Salad olivier (Page 60)
Mast-o-khiar ⓥ (Page 73)

Main course

Tahchin-e-bademjan (Page 91)
Khoresh-e-bademjan with polo (Page 107)

Dessert

Yakh dar behesht (Page 137)
Fresh fruit and ice cream

Saffron tea

Party Menu Five

Starter

Dolmeh kalam (Page 80)

Salad-e-karafs ⓥ (Page 72)

Main course

Loobia polo (Page 98)

Geymeh bademjan (Page 90)

Joojeh kebab (Page 116)

Dessert

Fereni ⓥ (Page 131)

Zoolbia and bamieh (Pages 122, 123)

Hazelnut coffee

Zoolbia and bamieh

Feast Menu One

Starter

Salad olivier (Page 60)
Green salad
Halim bademjan (Page 76)
Panir-o-sabzi (cheese and herbs)

Main course

Loobia polo (Page 98)
Morasaa polo (Page 92)
Geymeh bademjan (Page 90)
with polo (Page 84)
Tandoori chicken (Page 118)

Dessert

Nan-e-khamehi (Page 132)
Zoolbia and bamieh ⓥ (Pages 122, 123)
Shirberenj (Page 127)

Feast Menu Two

Starter

Coocoo sabzi ⓥ (Page 68)
Kashk-e-bademjan ⓥ (Page 66)
Green salad
Panir-o-sabzi (cheese and herbs)

Main course

Shevid bagali polo with lamb ⓥ (Page 94)
Khoresh-e-gormeh sabzi with polo (Page 113)
Joojeh kebab (Page 116)
Havig polo ⓥ (Page 101)

Dessert

Tarhalva ⓥ (Page 136)
Masgati ⓥ (Page 130)
Cream roulette (Page 134)

Feast Menu Three

Starter

Borani-e-esfenag ⓥ (Page 62)

Coocoo bademjan ⓥ (Page 65)

Salad-e-karafs ⓥ (Page 72)

Panir-o-sabzi (cheese and herbs)

Main course

Tahchin-e-bademjan (Page 91)

Khoresh-e-fesenjan with polo (Page 110)

Adas polo ⓥ (Page 96)

Chicken with aloo (Page 117)

Dessert

Sholezard ⓥ (Page 128)

Spicy apple dessert ⓥ (Page 126)

Yakh dar behesht ⓥ (Page 137)

Borani-e-esfenag

Starters

Ash-e-mast

Ingredients

Rice	1 cup
Sabzi ash	3 cups (fresh), 1 cup (dried)
Yellow split peas	1/2 cup
Onion	1 large
Butter	100g
Chicken breast	2 halves
Yoghurt	500ml carton

Preparation

Remove all skin from the chicken breast and put it in a large saucepan, chop the onion and add it to the chicken with 4 cups of water, salt and pepper, the yellow split peas and rice that you have washed well before. Simmer until the chicken is cooked, then take the breasts out and add the sabzi (if you are using dry sabzi it must be cooked with the chicken) and 3 cups of water (the mixture should be quite watery), then cook on a low temperature for at least half an hour. If you are using dried herbs it needs more time and more water that you can add as required.

Chop the chicken breasts finely and return them to the pan. When the ash is well blended together take it off the heat and add the yoghurt. Serve it in a bowl decorated with a little yoghurt, saffron and mint sauce.

Ash-e-jo

Ingredients

Sabzi ash .... 3 cups
Pearl barley .... 1 cup
Rice .... 1/2 cup
Lentils .... 1/2 cup
Cannellini beans .... 1/2 cup
Onion .... 2 large
Kashk (dried strained yogurt) .... 3 cups
Butter 100g
Lamb's neck 1kg
Saffron .... 1 teaspoon
Salt & pepper to taste

Preparation

All the dried ingredients like lentils and beans, rice and barley should be soaked the night before. In a large saucepan put the lamb's neck with one onion (chopped), salt and pepper and saffron. Add 6 cups of water and cook until the lamb is tender. Take the lamb out and add all the soaked ingredients to the juice that is left. Cook on a low temperature until they are all well cooked, you may need to add more water and stir occasionally, there should be enough water so that everything is swimming in it. Then add the sabzi (if the herbs are not fresh you can use dried herbs but in that case the herbs should be cooked with the rest of the ingredients). Chop the second onion and fry until golden, put half in the bean mixture and keep the rest for decoration. Once everything is cooked you can add the butter and the kashk, just keep 3 spoons of kashk for decorating the ash. Take all the meat from the bone and add it to the mixture, boil it for a few more minutes and transfer it into a large bowl. Decorate the top with fried onion, kashk and a little saffron.

Salad olivier

Ingredients

Potatoes .... 4 large
Chicken breasts 3
Green peas (small) .... 1 can
Salty gherkins .... 1 can
Eggs .... 3 hard-boiled
Lemon juice .... 4 tablespoons
Salt & pepper to taste
Olive oil .... 1/2 cup
Bay leaves 3
Olives .... 1/2 cup
Mayonnaise .... 2 cups
Fresh mint to decorate

Preparation

Take the skin off and cook the chicken breasts in 1/2 cup of water, salt and pepper and the bay leaves. Leave to cool. Cook the potatoes, chop into small pieces, and allow to cool down. Chop the chicken, eggs and gherkins finely, mix them all in a large bowl then add the peas. In a jar put the lemon juice, salt, pepper and olive oil, and shake it well then add it to the mixture. Then add 2/3 of the mayonnaise to the mixture and mix it well (you may put some fresh cream in this if you like, it certainly makes it tastier). Put it all in a shallow bowl and arrange it like a little hill, then put the rest of the mayonnaise on top and spread it all over evenly until it is covered. You may need more mayonnaise to cover. Then decorate it with gherkins, olives and fresh mint or parsley.

Borani-e-bademjan

Ingredients

Aubergines .... 4 medium
Onions .... 2 large
Dried mint .... 3 tablespoons
Yoghurt .... 1 large carton (500ml)
Oil .... 1 cup
Saffron powder .... 1 teaspoon
Salt & pepper to taste

Preparation

Chop the onions and fry them until golden. Peel the aubergines and cut them into 2cm rings and fry them on both sides. Put the aubergines, half the onions, saffron, salt and pepper in a pan with 1 cup of water and cook it slowly until the water evaporates. Let it cool down then mix it with a fork and add the yoghurt. Put it in a shallow bowl and decorate it with the rest of the onions, a little yoghurt and on top spread the fried mint (to fry the mint in a small frying pan heat 2 spoons of oil, add the mint and take it off the heat immediately). This dish can be served hot or cold.

Borani-e-esfenag

Ingredients

Spinach 500g
Yoghurt .... 1 large carton (500ml)
Salt & pepper to taste

Preparation

Wash the spinach well, place it in a saucepan and cook it for 10 minutes on a very low heat or steam it for a very short time, then put it in a colander and let the water drain from it while it cools. Put the yoghurt in a large bowl, add the salt and pepper and mix it well. Cut the spinach into smaller pieces and mix it with the yoghurt. Serve in a shallow bowl and decorate it with some of the yoghurt, sprinkled with paprika, fresh mint and radishes.

Chicken wings

Ingredients

Chicken wings 1kg
Flour .... 1 cup
Tandoori powder .... 3 tablespoons
Oil enough to deep fry
Fresh parsley and chilli to decorate

Preparation

Cut the top bit off the wings and cut them again on the joint. Wash and dry them, put the flour and the tandoori powder in a bowl and dip the wings in it, making sure the wings are all covered with the flour mixture. Heat the oil and fry the wings a few at a time. When they are all fried arrange them on a plate and decorate with parsley and fresh chilli.

Coocoo bademjan

Ingredients

Aubergines .... 4 medium
Eggs 5
Onion .... 1 large
Saffron .... 1/2 teaspoon
Oil .... 1 cup
Flour .... 2 tablespoons

Preparation

Peel the aubergines, then grate them on a large grater. Fry them in half the oil. Chop the onion and fry it separately. In a bowl break the eggs and add the salt and pepper, flour and saffron that you have mixed with a spoonful of water. Add the aubergine and onion and mix them well. In a large frying pan heat the rest of the oil, pour in the mixture, spread it evenly and lower the heat. Cover the top and let it set. When it is set cut it into six or eight portions and turn them over to fry the other side. When the other side is fried arrange the coocoo in a round dish and decorate with radishes and parsley.

Kashk-e-bademjan

Ingredients

Small aubergines	12
Onions	2 large
Oil	2 cups
Walnuts	1 cup
Dried mint	3 tablespoons
Kashk (dried strained yogurt)	2 cups
Garlic	5 cloves
Salt	1 tablespoon
Saffron	1/2 teaspoon

Preparation

Peel the aubergines place them on a tray and sprinkle one tablespoon of salt on them. Leave them for a few minutes while you chop the onion and garlic and fry them separately and put them aside. Heat 3 tablespoons of oil on a low temperature and put the dried mint in and immediately take it off the stove. Dab the aubergines with a kitchen tissue and then fry them whole, turning them so that all sides get fried. Put them in a shallow pan and add a cup of water, half the fried onions and half the fried garlic, saffron and pepper to taste (do not add any salt as kashk is salty.) Cook for about 15 minutes, then add the kashk and cook it for a further 5 to 10 minutes. Arrange the aubergines in a shallow bowl, pour the rest of the kashk on top, then decorate it with the rest of the fried onion, garlic and mint, and sprinkle the crushed walnuts on top.

Coocoo sabzi

Ingredients

4 herbs: parsley, Persian leek, coriander, and dill, chopped.......4 cups
Eggs.......4 large
Flour.......2 tablespoons
Salt.......1/2 teapoon
Pepper.......1/2 teaspoon
Zereshk (small sour berries).......1/2 cup
Walnuts.......1/2 cup
Oil.......1 cup

Preparation

Fry the chopped herbs in half of the oil and let them cool. Break the eggs in a large bowl, add the flour, salt and pepper and beat them together, then add the herbs, zereshk, walnuts and mix well. In a large non-stick frying pan heat the rest of the oil. When hot put the mixture in and quickly spread it evenly, lower the heat and simmer for about 15 minutes. When the whole of the coocoo is almost cooked (it should be set) cut it into six or eight pieces with a pizza knife then turn them over and fry the other side. It will not take more than 15 minutes, but if you like it well done leave it a bit longer. Do not cover it again so it stays crispy. Serve in a round dish and decorate with fresh mint.

Onion soup

Ingredients

Onions .... 2 large
Butter 100g
Tomato juice .... 2 cups
Single cream 200ml
Salt and pepper to taste
Stock cube 1
Fresh coriander .... 1 cup (chopped)
Flour .... 2 tablespoons

Preparation

Grate the onions with a medium grater. Melt the butter in a large saucepan and fry the onions for a few minutes, then add the flour and fry a little longer. Then add the tomato juice, salt and pepper and crumble the stock cube in. Pour in 6 cups of water and cook it slowly, stirring occasionally, until it thickens, then add the cream and coriander and serve immediately.

Koofteh-e-shevid bagali

Ingredients

Minced lamb or beef 500g
Fresh dill weed (chopped) .... 1 cup
Broad beans (peeled) .... 4 cups
Rice .... 1 cup
Eggs 3
Saffron .... 1/2 teaspoon
Flour .... 2 tablespoons
Onion .... 1 medium
Butter 100g

Preparation

Soak the rice for a few hours. Chop the dill weed, then mix the rice, broad beans, mince, saffron, eggs, salt, pepper and flour together using your hands. Make balls the size of tennis balls then melt the butter in a large saucepan and arrange the balls all next to each other (you should not put them on top of each other). Put the onion that you have fried before on top of the balls, add 4 cups of water and cook slowly on a low heat for about an hour. Keep checking the juice: you may have to add more water if it goes too dry. Depending on the rice used the cooking time may need to be a bit longer, but check the inside with a knife to see if the middle is cooked. This dish may be served with yoghurt.

Salad-e-karafs

Ingredients

Celery .... 1 medium head
Apples .... 2 large
Sultanas .... 1 cup
Walnuts .... 1 cup
Lemon .... 1 medium
Mayonnaise .... 1/2 cup
Olive oil .... 1/2 cup
Salt & pepper to taste

Preparation

Clean the celery stalks and cut them into one centimetre pieces. Cut the apple into small cubes and put them all in a large bowl, then add the sultanas and chopped walnuts. In a small jar put the lemon juice, olive oil and mayonnaise, salt and pepper and shake well, then add it to the salad. You can add some fresh cream to this salad if you want.

Mast-o-khiar

Ingredients

Full fat Greek yoghurt ....2 large (500ml) cartons
Cucumber..1 large
Fresh mint ....1 small bunch
Garlic ....2 cloves
Sultanas ....1 cup
Fresh cream (single) ....1 small carton
Salt & pepper to taste

Preparation

Peel the cucumber and chop it finely. Chop the mint (saving a little for decoration) and garlic. Put the yoghurt in a large bowl and beat it until smooth then add all the chopped ingredients, sultanas, cream, salt and pepper. Mix it well and serve in a bowl decorated with fresh mint.

Vegetarian

Nargesi

Ingredients

Spinach 500g
Eggs 4-6
Oil ....1 cup
Onion ....1 large
Salt & pepper to taste

Preparation

Wash and drain the spinach. Chop the onion and fry until golden, then add the spinach and fry for a further two minutes, then spread it wide in the frying pan, break the eggs in the middle and spinkle the salt and pepper on top. Cover it and cook on a low heat for five minutes, then serve.

Halim bademjan

Ingredients

Aubergines ....4 medium
Leg of lamb 500g
Lentils ....1 cup
Onions ....2 large
Garlic......................................5 cloves
Kashk ....2 cups
Oil ....1 cup
Saffron......................................1 teaspoon
Salt & pepper to taste

Preparation

Clean the lamb and take all the fat off, place it in a medium saucepan with one chopped onion, lentils, pepper (no salt as the kashk is normally very salty) and 4 cups of water. Cook until the meat is well cooked. Chop the other onion, garlic and fry them until golden. Peel and cube the aubergines and fry them until they are soft. Then add the saffron, fried onions and aubergines to the cooked meat and mash them all together until all the lumps disappear. Add the kashk and mix it well–check the saltiness at this stage to make sure it is all right. Cook the mixture on a very low heat for another 15 minutes and then tranfer it to a shallow dish, decorate it with the fried onions, garlic and kashk with a little saffron on top. This dish can be served cold or hot.

Shami

Ingredients

Minced lamb or meat	500g
Ground chick peas	2 cups
Onions	2 medium
Baking powder	1 teaspoon
Eggs	2
Saffron	1 teaspoon
Breadcrumbs	2 cups
Oil	2 cups
Fresh mint and parsley	a few bunches
Tomatoes, for decoration	

Preparation

Mince the onion or grate it finely, then mix it with the ground chick peas, salt and pepper and baking powder with 1/2 cup of water, then add the mince and saffron and mix it well until it is very smooth. Take a small amount of the mixture and make it into a round flat shape, then make a hole in the middle and cover it with breadcrumbs. Repeat until all the mixture is finished. Heat the oil and fry the shamis in a large frying pan. Arrange them in a dish and decorate with fresh mint, parsley and tomatoes.

Cutlet

Ingredients

Minced lamb or beef 500g
Potatoes ....8 large
White bread, crusts removed ....10 slices
Milk 280ml
Onion ....1 large
Oil for frying as needed
Breadcrumbs ....2 cups
Eggs 2
Saffron ....1 teaspoon
Salt & pepper to taste

Preparation

Cook 4 large potatoes and mash them. Grate the onion finely and put it in a large bowl with the mince, mashed potatoes, salt and pepper and saffron. Soak the bread in the milk and when it is soft squeeze out the excess milk. Mash the bread and add it to the mince mixture, then add the eggs and mix them all together well. Take a small amount of the mixture (about the size of a golf ball) and make a flat oval shape about 1 cm thick; cover it with breadcrumbs. Repeat this until you finish the mixture. Then heat the oil in a large frying pan and fry the cutlets on both sides. With the rest of the potatoes make long thin chips and arrange the cutlets and chips in a dish. Decorate it with tomatoes and parsley.

Dolmeh kalam

Ingredients

Rice .... 1 cup
Minced lamb or beef 250g
Yellow split peas .... 1 cup
Zereshk (small sour berries) .... 1/2 cup
Onion .... 1 large
White cabbage .... 1 medium
Sugar .... 1/2 cup
Lemon, juice of .... 1 large
Tomato juice .... 1 litre
Oil .... 1/2 cup
Salt & pepper to taste

Preparation

Separate the cabbage leaves, fill a large pan to 1/3 with water and bring to the boil. Put the cabbage leaves in and leave for 2 to 3 minutes, then take them out and let them cool down. Chop the onion and fry until golden. Add the mince and fry until brown. In a small pan cook the rice and split peas– the water you cook them in should be about one centimetre above the rice and peas in the pan. Cook slowly until the water is absorbed then add the meat and onions to the rice. Add the salt and pepper and zereshk and mix them all together. In every cabbage leaf put enough of the mixture so the leaf can be wrapped completely around it. Arrange the wrapped leaves with the gathered side down in a shallow pan so they are all on one level and not on top of each other, then mix the tomato juice, lemon juice and sugar with the oil and spread it on the leaves. Cook on a low temperature for about an hour, checking all the time that the juice does not run out– add some water if the juice gets too low. When dolmeh is ready it can be served in a shallow dish decorated with parsley and spring onions.

Coocoo shevid bagali

Ingredients

Broad beans ....3 cups
Fresh dill ....2 cups
Eggs 5
Onion 1
Oil ....1 cup
Salt & pepper to taste

Preparation

Take the skin off the broad beans and boil them for 2 to 3 minutes. Chop the onion and fry. Just before it turns golden, add the chopped dill, take it off the heat and let it cool down. In a large bowl break the eggs and beat them with the salt and pepper. Add the dill mixture and the broad beans and mix. In a medium non-stick frying pan heat the oil, spread the mixture in the pan and flatten it smoothly. Lower the temperature and cover for about 8 to 10 minutes. Check if it is set then cut into 6 portions and fry the other side. Serve on a plate and decorate with fresh mint and radishes.

Main Courses

How to cook rice

Rice must be washed thoroughly with cold water until the water runs clear, then soaked with plenty of salt (about 6 tablespoons). Ideally you should soak the rice overnight but 3 to 4 hours will be sufficient. Fill a large saucepan with water and bring to the boil, then add the soaked rice. Wait until it starts to boil then lower the temperature. Boil on medium heat and keep checking until the rice is long but not too soft. You can stir the rice very slowly with a wooden spoon, being very careful not to break the rice. Check that the rice is cooked by tasting it. It should not be hard in the middle but if you are not sure it is better if the rice is undercooked than overcooked. When it is ready pour the whole of the rice and water into a colander and let all the water drain out. Taste the rice for saltiness; if too salty pour some cold water over it and let it drain.

Put a glass of water in the saucepan and add 3 to 4 tablespoonfuls of oil and bring to the boil. Put half of the liquid aside and leave the rest in the saucepan, put all the rice in and, with the end of a spoon, make a few holes in the rice to breath. Cover and cook on a medium temperature until steam starts coming out of the rice, then add the rest of the oil and water. Cover the lid with a towel and reduce the heat to very low. Cook for 1/2 to 1 hour. You should get a nice fluffy rice. By experimenting you can get the feel of the rice that you are using, as different rices are cooked differently – some need more boiling and some less.

Sabzi polo

Ingredients

Mixed herbs .... 3 cups
Rice .... 4 cups
Salt .... 6 tablespoons
Onion .... 1 large
Oil .... 1/2 cup

Preparation

This is exactly like plain polo, but while the rice is boiling add the herbs and chopped onion. Boil until the rice is cooked, drain it in the colander, prepare the oil and water and cook as with plain rice. The only difference is that sabzi polo has to be boiled less than normal polo and the rice should be a bit hard when you drain it. If the rice was not cooked enough you can add a little more water to the oil and water that you put on top of the rice.

Mahi

Ingredients

How to prepare the fish for sabzi polo mahi

Grey or red mullet .... 2 large
Saffron .... 2 teaspoons
Lemons .... 4 large
Garlic .... 4 cloves
Plain flour .... 1 cup
Oil .... 2 cups
Salt & pepper to taste

Preparation

Clean the fish inside and out very well, take off all the scales and the fins but not the skin. Cut off the head and the tail too. Cut each fish into 5 equal pieces, sprinkle with salt and set it aside. In a bowl mix the flour with salt and pepper. Heat the oil in a large frying pan, put each piece of fish in the flour mixture to cover it well, then put it in the oil and fry each side. When all the pieces have been fried lower the heat and mix the juice of the lemons with the saffron and slowly put it in spoonfuls over the fish. Then turn the fish and fry them further until they are crispy all over. Serve with sabzi polo, and decorate the fish with parsley and cut lemons.

Zereshk polo

Ingredients

Zereshk (small sour berries)..................2 cups
Rice ....4 cups
Onions ....2 large
Salt ....6 tablespoons
Saffron Powder ....2 teaspoons
Lemon...1
Sugar ....5 tablespoons

Preparation

Soak the saffron in a cup with 3 tablespoons of hot water. Chop the onion finely and fry until golden, lower the temperature and add the zereshk (you can add a cup of dried cranberries too), then very quickly add the sugar and juice of the lemon. When it starts to boil add the saffron and put it aside. After draining the rice as before and preparing the oil and water, add a little saffron to the half that is left in the pan and cook as normal. When serving, spread the zereshk mixture in or on top of the rice.

Tahchin-e-bademjan

Ingredients

Rice	500g
Lamb	1kg leg
Aubergines	3 medium
Yoghurt	1 large carton
Eggs	2
Saffron	2 teaspoons
Oil	1 cup
Onion	1 large
Salt and pepper to taste	

Preparation

Boil the lamb with the onion, salt and pepper and with 3 cups of water until tender. There should be very little juice left. Leave to cool. Peel the aubergines and cut into 2cm circles then fry them until golden, leave to cool. Put the yoghurt in a large bowl and add the eggs, saffron, salt and pepper to taste. Cut the cooked lamb into small pieces and mix with 1/3 of the yoghurt mixture. Cook the rice as normal, drain and mix it with the rest of the yoghurt mixture. In a large non-stick saucepan put half the oil, then a quarter of the rice and yoghurt mixture and flatten it, then arrange the aubergines all over the rice so the rice is covered, then put another quarter of the rice on top and flatten gently, do not press. Now arrange the lamb all over, and lastly put the rest of the rice on and flatten it. Make several holes in the rice, cover the pan, and cook on a medium heat until steam comes out of the rice. Take about half a cup of the meat juice and pour it on top of the rice, cover it with a towel round the lid, then reduce the temperature to low and cook for 45 minutes to one hour. To serve this dish you need to turn it over into a round dish and cut it like a cake. This dish can be made with chicken (boneless) instead of lamb or spinach instead of aubergine.

Morasaa polo

Ingredients

Orange peel .... 1/2 cup
Rice .... 3 cups
Saffron .... 2 teaspoons
Zereshk (small sour berries) .... 1 cup
Sultanas .... 1 cup
Chopped almonds .... 1/2 cup
Chopped pistachios .... 1/2 cup
Butter 200g
Chicken .... 1 medium
Onion .... 1 large
Salt and pepper to taste

Preparation

Clean the chicken and cook it in a pan with 1/2 cup of water and the onion. When it is cooked take all the bones and skin off and leave the meat in the pan to stay warm. Prepare the rice and cook exactly as polo (plain rice), then soak the saffron in 3 spoons of hot water and leave it to cool. In a small frying pan melt 2 spoons of butter and on a low heat slightly fry the zereshk. Then add 2 teaspoons of saffron and put it aside. Repeat this with the sultanas, almonds, orange peel and pistachios, keeping them all warm in separate bowls. When the rice is ready to serve put some in the dish and spread the chicken all over it, then put the rest of the rice on the top. Do not fill too much as you need room for the other ingredients. Then decorate it with all the fried ingredients all over the top.

Shevid bagali polo

Ingredients

Rice .... 3 cups
Broad beans .... 2 cups
Dill weed .... 2 cups
Salt .... 5 tablespoons
Butter or oil .... 1 cup

Preparation

Wash and soak the rice as usual, take the skin off the broad beans and chop the dill. Fill a large pan up to a 1/3 with water and bring to the boil, then add the rice and just before the rice is ready add the broad beans and dill weed. Boil until the rice is ready and then drain in a colander. Taste to make sure it is not too salty (if it is too salty pour some water over it to wash the salt out). Put half the oil or butter in a pan with 1 cup of water. Add the rice and make holes in it with a spoon. Put it on a medium heat for 15 minutes then add the rest of the oil and water mixture and cover the lid with a towel to steam the rice for 1/2 an hour, then serve with chicken or lamb.

Adas polo

Ingredients

Rice....4 cups
Lentils....2 cups
Sultanas....1 cup
Dried cranberries....1 cup
Dates (stoned)....2 cups
Saffron....1/2 teaspoon
Salt....6 tablespoons
Butter....100g

Preparation

Lentils can be soaked or not – they take less time to cook if soaked. Cook them then run under cold water and drain. Boil the rice as normal and just before draining add the lentils and drain together. Add a teaspoon of hot water to the saffron and leave it for a while. In a frying pan melt the butter on a low heat, fry the sultanas and cranberries in it then add half the saffron. Fry the dates separately. After you halve the oil and water for the rice add the rest of the saffron to the half that is left in the pan, then put the rice and lentils in and steam until cooked. When ready to serve put the rice in a dish and decorate it with the sultanas, cranberries and dates.

Loobia polo

Ingredients

Basmati rice	500g
Salt	5 tablespoons
Oil	200g
Onion	1 large
Leg of lamb	1kg
French beans	1kg
Tomato puree	2 tablespoons
Pepper	1 teaspoon
Saffron	$\frac{1}{2}$ teaspoon
Polo spice (available at selected stores)	2 tablespoons

Preparation

Clean the French beans and cut into 2cm lengths. Chop the onions and, using $\frac{1}{4}$ of the oil, fry with the beans. Take off all the fat from the lamb, cut it into small cubes and fry with $\frac{1}{4}$ of the oil, then add it to the fried beans. Add 1 tablespoon of salt, pepper, saffron and the tomato puree and one cup of water and simmer slowly for half an hour. Cook the rice as on p. 84. After you drain it prepare the oil and water as before and put half of it in the pan, then put $\frac{1}{4}$ of the rice in, spread it flat then put half of the meat mixture in. Again flatten it but do not press hard. Sprinkle half of the spices on top and repeat one layer of rice and the rest of the meat mixture, finishing with the last of the rice. Sprinkle the last of the spices on top, make holes and cook as normal rice. When serving, mix the rice and sauce as you dish it out. This dish can be cooked with mince instead of diced lamb.

Eslamboli polo

Ingredients

Basmati rice 500g
Oil .... 1 cup
Chopped tomatoes 500g
Aubergines .... 2 medium, cubed
Saffron powder .... 1 teaspoon
Potato .... 1 large
Salt & Pepper to taste

Preparation

Wash the rice in cold water and rinse a few times until the water runs clear. Leave to soak in enough water to cover the rice, along with 4 tablespoons of salt. Heat 2 tablespoons of oil, add aubergine cubes and fry well. Add chopped tomatoes, one teaspoon of salt, pepper and saffron. Cook for 5 minutes. Half fill a large pan with water, bring to the boil, then add the soaked rice and boil at a low temperature. The rice should be half cooked when put in a sieve to drain. Put about half a glass of water in a big pan, add the rest of the oil and bring to the boil. Put half of it aside and leave the rest in the pan. At this stage you can put sliced potatoes at the bottom and then put half the rice in. Flatten it, add the aubergine and tomato sauce, then the rest of the rice. Make holes with the end of a spoon for the rice to breath and cook on a medium heat for 20 minutes. Then pour the rest of the oil and water on the rice, cover the lid with a towel and leave to steam for another half an hour. When ready turn it over into a dish and cut in slices to serve.

Havig polo

Ingredients

Rice.........3 cups
Carrots.........1kg
Zereshk (small sour berries).........1 cup
Onion.........1 large
Oil.........1 cup
Saffron.........3 teaspoons
Sugar.........5 tablespoons
Lemon.........1 large
Salt & pepper to taste

Preparation

Wash and soak the rice in salted water for at least 2 hours. Chop the onions and fry until golden. Clean the carrots and cut them into strips, then add them to the onions and fry them together. When the carrots are cooked lower the temperature and add the zereshk, turn them a few times then add the sugar, the juice of the lemon and half of the saffron. Cook for a few minutes and it is ready. Boil the rice as for polo and drain it in a large sieve. Check the saltiness, and rinse with cold water if it is too salty. Prepare the oil and water as before and leave half in the saucepan. Put in 1/3 of the rice, flatten it, then put in 1/2 the carrot mixture and again flatten it lightly. Repeat with another layer of rice and the rest of the carrot mixture, then the remaining rice on top. Make several holes in the rice, cover and cook on a medium heat for 10 minutes. Add the rest of the oil mixture, cover with a towel round the lid and reduce the temperature to low, for 1/2 an hour to 45 minutes. When serving, the rice and the carrots have to be mixed lightly in the pan.

Saffron chicken or lamb

Ingredients

Chicken....................1 medium
 or lamb....................½ leg
Onion....................1 large
Saffron....................½ teaspoon
Butter....................100g
Salt & pepper to taste

Preparation

Put the chicken or lamb in a medium pan with the chopped onion and water: chicken needs 1 cup of water but lamb needs about three cups. Add salt and pepper and cook on a medium heat: 20 minutes for chicken, about 45 minutes for lamb. When the meat is cooked add the saffron and butter and cook for another 5 to 10 minutes. Serve with any rice that you like.

Chicken in tomato sauce

Ingredients

Chicken...1 medium
Onion ....1 large
Chopped tomatoes 500g
Garlic ....3 cloves
Oil ....4 tablespoons
Salt and pepper to taste

Preparation

Clean the chicken and remove the skin if you want to. Cut the chicken into 8 to 10 pieces. Chop the onion and the garlic and fry them in the oil. Take out the onion and garlic and fry the chicken in the remaining oil until brown. Add the onion, garlic, salt and pepper, and tomatoes to the pan. A little water might be helpful if you feel the mixture is dry. Let it cook on a medium heat for about half an hour or until the chicken is tender. You can serve this chicken with different types of rice, or french fries.

Kalam polo

Ingredients

Small white cabbage 1
Minced lamb 500g
Rice .... 3 cups
Salt & pepper to taste
Onion .... 1 large
Mixed spice .... 4 teaspoons
Oil .... 1 cup

Preparation

Chop the onion and fry in oil until golden. Put aside and fry the mince well (you can use lamb or beef). Chop the cabbage into small pieces and fry in a separate frying pan, then add the fried onion and mince with salt and pepper and 2 teaspoons of mixed spice. A little lemon juice will add taste to it as well, add half a cup of water and cook slowly for 15 minutes.
Prepare the rice as for polo and drain. Prepare the oil and water and, to the half that remains in the pan, add 2 teaspoons of mixed spice and then 1/3 of the rice. Next comes half the mince mixture then another 1/3 of rice, then the rest of the mince, and finally the rest of the rice. Make holes in the rice and cook as normal. This polo has to be cooked slowly as the bottom burns easily so give it a little more time. You can also spread some more of the mixed spice on top of the rice.

Geymeh bademjan

Ingredients

Lamb 1kg
Aubergines .... 4 medium
Yellow split peas .... 1 cup
Onion .... 1 large
Tomato puree .... 3 tablespoons
Oil .... 2 cups
Salt & pepper to taste
Saffron

Preparation

Peel the aubergines and cut them in half lengthways. Sprinkle with a little salt and leave for 1/2 to 1 hour. Clean the lamb of all fat and cut it into about 1 to 2cm cubes. Chop the onion and fry it in a large saucepan in 3 tablespoons of oil. Add the lamb and fry for 10 minutes, then add the tomato paste and mix well. Add the split peas, 4 cups of water, salt and pepper and saffron then cook on a medium heat for half an hour. Check all the time that it does not burn, add more water if it gets dry. When the lamb is tender it should be in about 2 cups of water. Fry the aubergines on both sides in the rest of the oil and put them on top of the cooked lamb. Continue to cook on a low heat for 15 minutes. When serving, put the aubergines around the edge of a shallow bowl and the meat in the middle. This dish can be made without aubergine and instead fry very thin slices of potatoes and spread these over the meat and split peas when you are serving the dish.

Khoresh-e-loobiasabz

Ingredients

String beans 1kg
Lamb or beef 1kg
Onion .... 1 large
Garlic .... 3 cloves
Salt & pepper to taste
Saffron .... 1 teaspoon
Chopped tomatoes .... 1 can
Lemon 1

Preparation

Remove all fat from the meat and cut it into 2cm cubes. Chop the onion and garlic and fry them in a medium saucepan, then add the meat and fry until the meat is cooked. Add the tomatoes, salt and pepper and saffron and cook until the meat is tender. Clean the beans and cut them into 2–3cm pieces and fry them in a frying pan. When the meat is cooked add the beans and the juice of the lemon (if you like you can add more lemon juice). Cook for 1/2 an hour and serve with rice. Do not overcook this khoresh as the beans will get mushy.

Khoresh-e-bademjan

Ingredients

Lamb or beef 1kg
Aubergines .... 4 medium
Tomatoes 500g
Limoo amani (dried lime) 6
Oil .... 2 cups
Onion .... 1 large
Garlic .... 3 cloves
Sour grapes (unripe grapes) .... 1 cup
Saffron .... 1 teaspoon
Salt and pepper to taste

Preparation

Take off all the fat from the meat and cut it into 3cm cubes. Chop the onion and garlic and fry in a medium saucepan until golden, then add the meat and fry again until the meat is browned. Add the salt and pepper, saffron and 3 cups of water and cook until the meat is tender – if you need you can add more water for the meat to cook. Peel the aubergines and cut them in half lengthways. Fry both sides in a frying pan. When the meat is ready arrange the aubergines on top and then cut the tomatoes in half and arrange them on top of the aubergines. Cook for 1/2 an hour then add the sour grapes and cook for a further 10 minutes and your khoresh is ready to serve. Arrange the aubergines around the edge of a shallow bowl, put the meat in the middle and the tomatoes on top of the aubergines; serve with rice.

Khoresh-e-karafs

Ingredients

Celery .... 1 large head
Lamb or beef 1kg
Fresh parsley .... 1 bunch
Fresh mint .... 1 bunch
Onion .... 1 large
Oil .... 2 cups
Lemons 2
Salt & pepper to taste
Turmeric .... 1 teaspoon

Preparation

Chop the onion and fry it in 1/2 a cup of oil until golden. Clean the celery stalks and cut them into 3 to 4cm pieces. Fry them in 1/2 cup of oil, then add the parsley and mint which you have previously chopped and fry for another 5 minutes, then put it aside. Take all the fat from the meat and cut it into 3 to 4cm cubes. Fry it in a medium size saucepan, then add the fried onions, salt and pepper, turmeric and 4 cups of water and cook until the meat is tender. You might need to add some more water. When the meat is ready add the celery and lemon juice and cook for a further 1/2 an hour until the celery is cooked but not overcooked. The khoresh is ready to be served with rice.

Koresh-e-fesenjan

Ingredients

Chicken breasts 4
Walnuts 1kg
Concentrated pomegranate juice .... 1 cup
Sugar .... 1 cup
Onion 1
Golpar (a dried herb) .... 1 teaspoon
Oil .... 1 cup
Saffron .... 1/2 teaspoon

Preparation

Take off all the skin and fat from the chicken and fry it in a saucepan along with the chopped onion. Add a cup of water, the saffron and golpar and cook for half an hour. Grind the walnuts finely and fry them slowly for 5 minutes as they burn easily. Add 3 cups of water, the salt and pepper and cook for half an hour, then add the concentrated pomegranate juice and sugar (some people do not like this khoresh sweet, in which case there is no need for sugar). Let it boil slowly, stirring it occasionally so that it does not burn at the bottom, then add the cooked chicken and let it boil for a further 5 to 10 minutes and serve it with rice.

Khoresh-e-alooesfenag

Ingredients

Lamb or beef 1kg
Spinach 1kg
Tomato puree .... 3 tablespoons
Onions .... 2 large
Garlic .... 3 cloves
Turmeric .... 1 teaspoon
Salt and pepper to taste
Aloo (dried peeled prunes) .... 2 cups
Oil .... 1 cup

Preparation

Take off all the fat from the meat and cut into 2cm cubes. Chop the onions and garlic and fry them until golden; put them aside to cool. Fry the spinach in half the oil for 2 to 3 minutes, then leave to cool. Fry the meat in the rest of the oil with the salt, pepper, turmeric and 2 cups of water until the meat is tender. There should not be a lot of juice as this khoresh is supposed to be quite dry. Then add the spinach, onion and garlic and cook for another 5 minutes. Serve with rice. It is very nice if you like hot food to put a little red chilli powder in to make it hot.

Khoresh-e-gormeh sabzi

Ingredients

Lamb or beef	1kg
Gormeh sabzi (4 herbs)	4 cups (2 cups if dried)
Red kidney beans	1 can (500g)
Onion	1 large
Limoo amani (dried limes)	6
Oil	2 cups
Salt and pepper to taste	
Turmeric	1 teaspoon

Preparation

Trim any fat from the meat and cut it into 2cm pieces. Chop the onion and fry it in a medium size saucepan until golden. Add the meat and fry well (if you are using dried herbs then you should add them to the meat at this stage and fry for a minute), then add salt and pepper, turmeric and 3 cups of water and cook until the meat is tender. If the herbs are fresh fry them in one cup of oil and add them to the cooked meat at this stage. With a fork make several holes in the limes and put them in with the meat and cook for 1/2 an hour. Put the kidney beans with the juice in and cook for a further 10 minutes. There should be just enough juice – not too watery. If there is too much juice then cook it a bit longer for the water to evaporate. Serve with plain rice.

Kebab-e-coobideh

Ingredients

Minced lamb..500 g
Onions ....2 medium
Salt & pepper to taste
Saffron ....½ teaspoon
Sumac (dried powdered herbs) ....½ cup

Preparation

Grate the onion, squeeze the juice out and add it to the minced lamb with the salt and pepper. Melt the saffron in 2 spoons of water and add it to the mince. Mix until it is really combined well, then either put it on skewers or just make into long, thin shapes and grill both sides. You can add the sumac while it is grilling. Serve with rice and kebab e barg.

Kebab-e-barg

Ingredients

Lamb fillet 1kg
Onions .... 2 large
Olive oil .... 5 tablespoons
Salt & pepper to taste
Sumac .... 1/2 cup
Small tomatoes 10 to12
Saffron .... 1/2 teaspoon

Preparation

The lamb fillet must be cleaned of all fat, then cut into 3 to 4cm widths. If it is thick cut it thinner. Place the meat in a bowl. Grate the onions and squeeze the juice out. Put the juice on the meat with salt, pepper and olive oil, then mix the saffron with 2 spoons of warm water and add it to the meat. Marinade it overnight. Kebabs and tomatoes should be put on skewers and grilled both sides and served with plain rice (polo). Usually we either serve on individual plates on which you put the rice first and the kebab on the side with grilled tomatoes, or the rice in a large dish and the kebabs with flat bread on top and grilled tomatoes on the side in another dish. If you like, the sumac can be spread on the kebabs.

Joojeh kebab

Ingredients

Small chickens 3
Onions ....2 medium
Olive oil ....1/2 cup
Salt & pepper to taste
Lemon juice ....3 tablespoons
Garlic ....2 cloves

Preparation

Clean the chickens and cut them into small pieces. Grate the onion and garlic and place them on the chicken. Add the olive oil and lemon juice and marinade it for at least 2 hours. Place all the chickens in a shallow tray and grill. When one side is done turn to the other side. When ready to serve decorate it with lemon slices and parsley.

Chicken with aloo

Ingredients

Chicken .... 1 medium
Onion .... 1 large
Garlic .... 2 cloves
Salt & pepper to taste
Aloo (dried peeled prunes) .... 2 cups
Saffron .... 1 teaspoon
Butter 100g

Preparation

Clean the chicken, take off the wings and the legs, then put it in a medium pan. Chop the onion and garlic and add to the pan with salt, pepper, saffron and 1 cup of water. Cook for 1/2 an hour. When the chicken is half cooked add the aloo and butter and cook it further until the aloo is quite soft. If you find it too sour you can add one or two spoons of sugar. This dish can be served with plain rice.

Tandoori chicken

Ingredients

Tandoori paste............2 to 4 spoons
Yoghurt............1 large carton
Lemon juice............3 tablespoons
Butter or margarine 100g
Chicken............1 medium

Preparation

Mix the yoghurt, tandoori paste and lemon juice together – do not add any salt or pepper as tandoori paste is hot and salty. Cut the chicken into pieces, take off all the skin, and marinade in the mixture (overnight if possible). Spread the chicken in a deep tray, dot with the butter, and cook in the oven for half an hour. When one side is cooked turn the chicken over and cook until the other side is done. Do not allow the chicken to go dry – add a little water if it does. Serve in a dish decorated with parsley, mint and radishes.

Desserts

Zoolbia

Ingredients

Arrowroot	500g
Water	3 tablespoons
Yoghurt	small carton
Oil enough for deep-frying	

Preparation

Mix the arrowroot with the water, then add the yoghurt and mix well until it is smooth. In a shallow pan heat the oil then put the mixture in a piping bag and squeeze it out slowly to make a round basket shape. Fry one side then the other and take it out to cool, repeat until the mixture is finished. Then drizzle with syrup (see page 124).

Vegetarian

Bamieh

Ingredients

Flour .... 1 cup
Water .... 1 cup
Oil .... 5 tablespoons
Eggs 3
Oil enough for deep-frying

Preparation

In a medium pan bring the water and oil to the boil, then add the flour and mix. It will become quite thick, then take it off the heat and let it cool a little. Add the eggs one by one and mix well in between until all the eggs are in and you have a very smooth mixture. Then heat the oil in a shallow pan, put the mixture in a piping bag and squeeze a little out at a time fry until golden. Take the shapes out and let them cool down. When all the mixture has been used, soak the bamieh well in syrup (see page 124) and serve.

Vegetarian

Syrup for Zoolbia & Bamieh

Ingredients

Sugar .... 2 cups
Water .... 1 cup
Rosewater .... 1/2 cup
Vanilla essence .... 1/2 teaspoon

Preparation

In a medium pan mix the sugar, water and rosewater and boil until it is quite thick, then add the vanilla essence. After 2 minutes take it off the heat. Can be used for both zoolbia and bamieh.

Spicy Apple Dessert

Ingredients

Golden Delicious apples........................6
Sugar ....2 cups
Cinnamon ....4 teaspoons
Butter ....3 tablespoons

Preparation

Peel the apples, quarter them and remove the cores. Cut them into half moon shapes. In a non-stick dish, put a spoonful of butter and warm it to melt, then arrange the apples neatly in one layer in the dish. Spread the sugar and cinnamon over the apples then put on another layer of apples and repeat with the sugar and cinnamon until the apples are all used, finishing with a topping of sugar and cinnamon. Spread the rest of the butter all over it and cook it in a medium heat oven for half an hour, making sure it does not burn. This dessert can be served hot or cold with cream or ice cream.

Shirberenj

Ingredients

Rice .... 1 cup
Milk .... 2.3 litres
Rosewater .... 1/2 cup
Single cream 280ml
Almond flakes .... 1 cup

Preparation

Wash the rice well with lots of water – it is good if the rice can be soaked for an hour or two. Then cook it with two cups of water until it is soft. Add the milk, rosewater and almond flakes and cook slowly until it thickens, then add the cream and pour it into dessert bowls and let it cool down. Shirberenj can be served on its own or with any favourite jam or honey.

Vegetarian

Sholezard

Ingredients

Rice 500g
Sugar 1kg
Oil .... 1 cup
Saffron .... 2 teaspoons
Rosewater .... 1 cup
Almond flakes .... 1 cup
Pistachios .... 1/2 cup
Cinnamon .... 3 teaspoons

Preparation

Wash the rice thoroughly. For each cup of rice add six cups of water to a large saucepan. Boil the rice until it becomes soft in the middle, then add the sugar and cook until it is thick and creamy. If it goes too thick add more water. Add the saffron that has been soaked in hot water, then warm the oil and add it to the mixture. Put 2/3 of the almonds in, along with the rosewater, mix it well then simmer for half an hour on a very low temperature. When ready, put it in a bowl and decorate it with the rest of the almonds, pistachios and cinnamon.

Vegetarian

Masgati

Ingredients

Arrowroot	1 cup
Sugar	2 cups
Water	6 cups
Rosewater	1 cup
Oil	1/2 cup
Almond flakes	1 cup
Ground almonds	1/2 cup
Ground pistachios	1/2 cup

Preparation

Mix the arrowroot with the water in a pan on a low heat and bring to the boil. Boil it until it is a little thick, then add the sugar, rosewater and the almond flakes. In a separate pan heat the oil, add it to the mixture, and mix it well until it is thick. Put the masgati in small serving bowls and decorate it with ground almonds and ground pistachios. This dessert is served cold.

Vegetarian

Fereni

Ingredients

Milk	1 pint
Ground rice	3 tablespoons
Sugar	1/2 cup
Rosewater	3 tablespoons
Ground almonds	1/2 cup
Ground pistachios	1/2 cup

Preparation

Mix the ground rice with the milk, sugar and rosewater in a pan and cook it on a low heat. Bring it to the boil, stirring all the time, until it is thick and creamy, then add the ground almonds and pistachios. Put the mixture in a shallow bowl and decorate with pistachios and almonds, let it cool and serve.

Vegetarian

Nan-e-khamehi

Ingredients

Water .... 1 cup
Flour .... 1 cup
Oil .... 4 tablespoons
Eggs 5
Sugar .... 2 teaspoons
Double cream .... 2 large cartons
Sugar for cream .... 1 cup
Rosewater .... 5 tablespoons

Preparation

In a medium pan put the water, oil and sugar and bring to the boil. Put all the flour in at once and mix it a little then take it off the heat and beat it until it is thick. Add the eggs one by one and mix it well: the mixture should be soft and creamy. Grease a baking tray and put small amounts of the mixture (it depends how big you want the éclairs to be) on the tray. Cook in a preheated oven on medium to high for half an hour then lower the temperature to medium and leave for 15 minutes. When they are golden they are ready. Let them cool down.
Beat the cream with the sugar and rosewater until it thickens, then cut the sides of the éclairs and empty the insides. Fill them with the cream mixture, place in a dish and decorate with icing sugar. (You can put crème anglais in the éclairs instead of cream).

Cream Roulette

Ingredients

Whipping cream ....2 large cartons
Eggs 10
Sugar..............................16 tablespoons
Flour..............................10 tablespoons
Vanilla sugar ....1 teaspoon
Rosewater ....3 spoons
Jam (strawberry or any other) ..1 jar
Grated chocolate for decoration

Preparation

Separate the egg yolks from the whites, put 10 spoonfuls of sugar and the vanilla sugar in with the egg yolks and beat them until they are almost white. In a separate bowl whisk the egg whites until they are stiff. Add the yolk mixture to the egg whites, then add the flour spoon by spoon and mix well. Grease a large non-stick baking tray and cover it with rice paper. Pour the mixture onto the tray – it should be about 1.5cm thick. Cook it in a preheated oven on a medium heat for 10 to 15 minutes, checking frequently that it doesn't burn. Once it is slightly golden it is ready. Take it out of the oven, peel off the rice paper and let it cool. Then take two clean J-cloths and dampen them. Spread one out and place the sponge cake on it. Then put the second J-cloth over the top and use it to help you roll the sponge up lengthways. Leave it in the fridge for about 2 hours. Put the whipping cream in a bowl, add the remainder of the sugar and the rosewater and whisk it until it is thick enough not to drop from a spoon. Unroll the sponge very carefully so that it doesn't break and spread the jam all over it. Then spread half of the cream on top of the jam and carefully roll it back up. Place it in the serving dish so that the seam of the roll is underneath, then decorate the top with the rest of the cream. Grate some chocolate over the top and leave it in the fridge for at least 2 hours before serving, otherwise it is too soft to cut.

Tarhalva

Ingredients

Flour	500g
Sugar	2 cups
Oil	2 cups
Saffron powder	3 teaspoons
Water	2 cups
Rosewater	1/2 cup
Ground pistachios	1/2 cup

Preparation

Put the oil in a medium pan and heat it, then add the flour and fry it slowly, stirring all the time until it is light brown. In a large bowl mix the water, sugar, rosewater and saffron together and warm it till the sugar is melted, then add it to the fried flour. Mix well until it starts looking oily, then spread the mixture in a dish and flatten it. You can make patterns on it as you like and decorate it with ground pistachios. This dish can be served hot or cold.

Yakh dar behesht

Ingredients

- Rice powder .... 1/4 cup
- Arrowroot .... 1/2 cup
- Sugar .... 1 1/2 cups
- Rosewater .... 1 tablespoon
- Milk .... 2 1/2 cups
- Water .... 2 cups
- Crushed pistachios .... 1/2 cup

Preparation

Mix the arrowroot and water and put it through a sieve to be smooth, then mix the rice powder with the milk and sieve that. In a medium pan mix the two together and cook on a low heat until it starts to boil, stirring all the time so it doesn't burn at the bottom. Cook until the mixture is quite thick then add the sugar and rosewater, stirring all the time until it is so thick that the spoon leaves an impression. Spread the mixture in a shallow dish (or in individual serving bowls) and let it cool down. When it is completely set you can cut it into square portions and decorate it with the crushed pistachios.

INDEX

Adas polo 40, 54, 96
Ash-e-jo 20, 59
Ash-e-mast 16, 58
Bamieh 38, 46, 50, 52, 123
Borani-e-bademjan 14, 30, 62
Borani-e-esfenag 26, 54, 63
Chicken in tomato sauce 18. 103
Chicken wings 28. 64
Chicken with aloo 54, 117
Coocoo bademjan 10, 47, 54, 65
Coocoo sabzi 8, 22, 46, 53, 68
Coocoo shevid bagali 49, 81
Cream roulette 16, 40, 48, 53, 134
Cutlet 40, 48, 78
Dolmeh kalam 50, 80
Eslamboli polo 18, 100
Fereni 28, 50, 131
Geymeh bademjan 47, 105
Halim bademjan 18, 36, 48, 52, 76
Havig polo 63, 10
Joojeh kebab 50, 53, 116
Kalam polo 42, 104
Kashk-e-bademjan 42, 53, 66
Khoresh-e-alooesfenag 32, 112
Khoresh-e-bademjan 26, 49, 107
Khoresh-e-barg 38, 115
Khoresh-e-coobideh 38, 114
Khoresh-e-fesenjan 30, 48, 54, 110
Khoresh-e-gormeh sabzi 24, 46, 53, 113
Khoresh-e-karafs 34, 48, 108
Khoresh-e-loobiasabz 28, 106
Koofteh-e-shevid bagali 24, 70
Loobia polo 14, 50, 52, 90
Mahi 16, 22, 87
Masgati 30, 34, 53, 130
Mast-o-khiar 8, 38, 43, 46, 48, 49, 73

Morasaa polo 47, 52, 92
Nan-e-khamehi 14, 48, 52, 132
Nargesi 34, 74
Onion soup 12, 69
Polo 10, 24, 36, 30, 32, 34, 46, 48, 52, 84
Sabzi polo 16, 22, 86
Saffron chicken or lamb 12, 40, 102
Salad-e-karafs 50, 54, 72
Salad olivier 46, 49, 52, 60
Shami 32, 47, 77
Shevid bagali polo 8, 36, 46, 53, 94
Shirberenj 10, 22, 47, 52, 127
Sholezard 20, 38, 42, 46, 54, 128
Spicy apple dessert 18, 26, 47, 54, 126
Syrup for zoolbia & bamieh 124
Tahchin-e-bademjan 20, 49, 54, 91
Tandoori chicken 14, 52, 118
Tarhalva 24, 32, 53, 136
Yakh dar behesht 36, 49, 54, 137
Zereshk polo 12, 88
Zoolbia 12, 38, 46, 50, 52, 122